AF576878

THE FINAL SEASON

THE FINAL SEASON

By

VIOLET TURNER

THE GOLDEN QUILL PRESS
Publishers
Francestown New Hampshire

Library of Congress Catalog Card Number 86-81283

ISBN 0-8233-0422-1

Printed in the United States of America

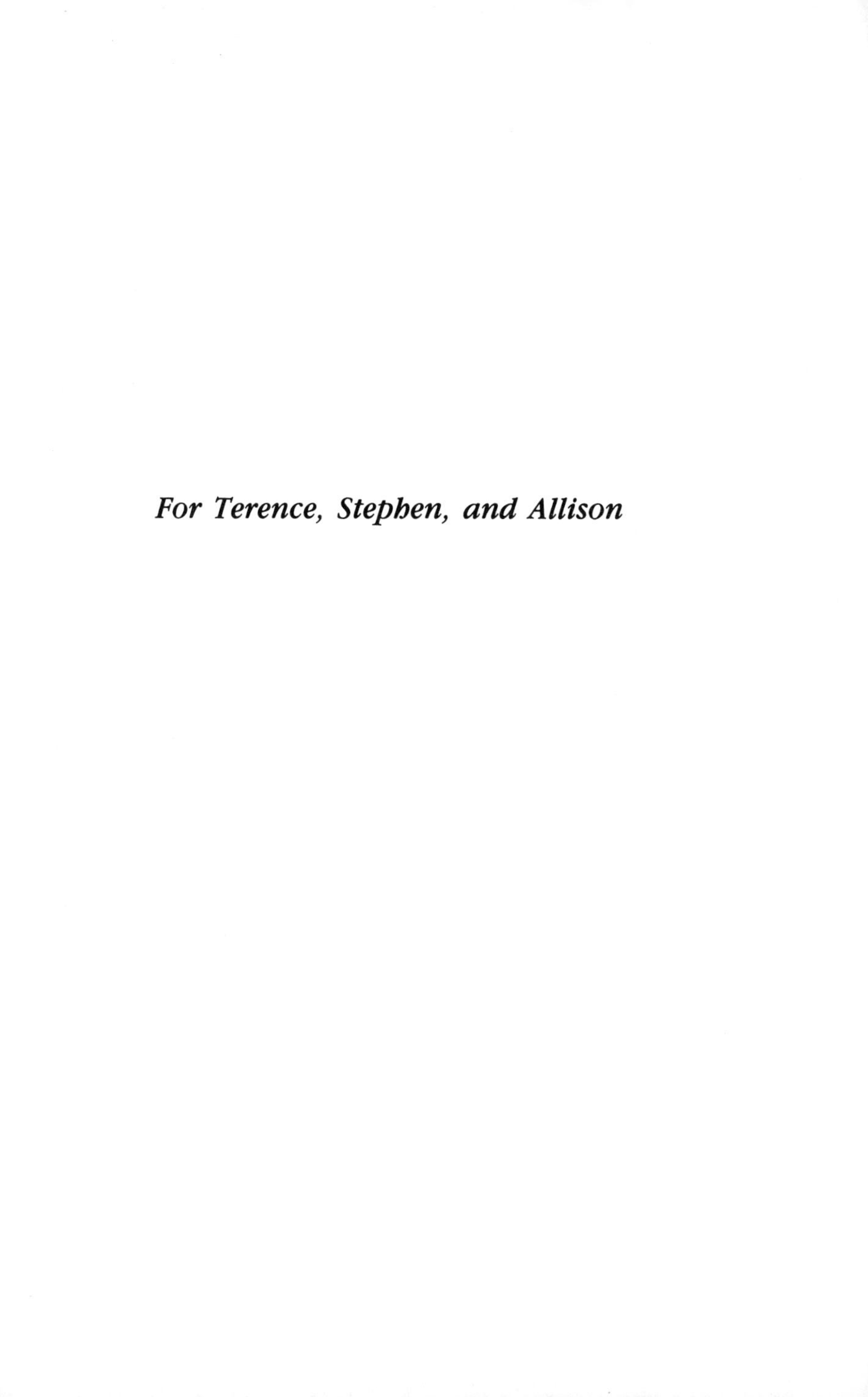

For Terence, Stephen, and Allison

ACKNOWLEDGMENTS

Grateful acknowledgment is made to *Poetry*, in which "Wild Bird" first appeared. Other poems have previously appeared in The Virginia Quarterly Review, Voices, and *The Washington Post.*

CONTENTS

AS THE EARTH TURNS

DOUBLE VISION

ASPECTS OF LOVE

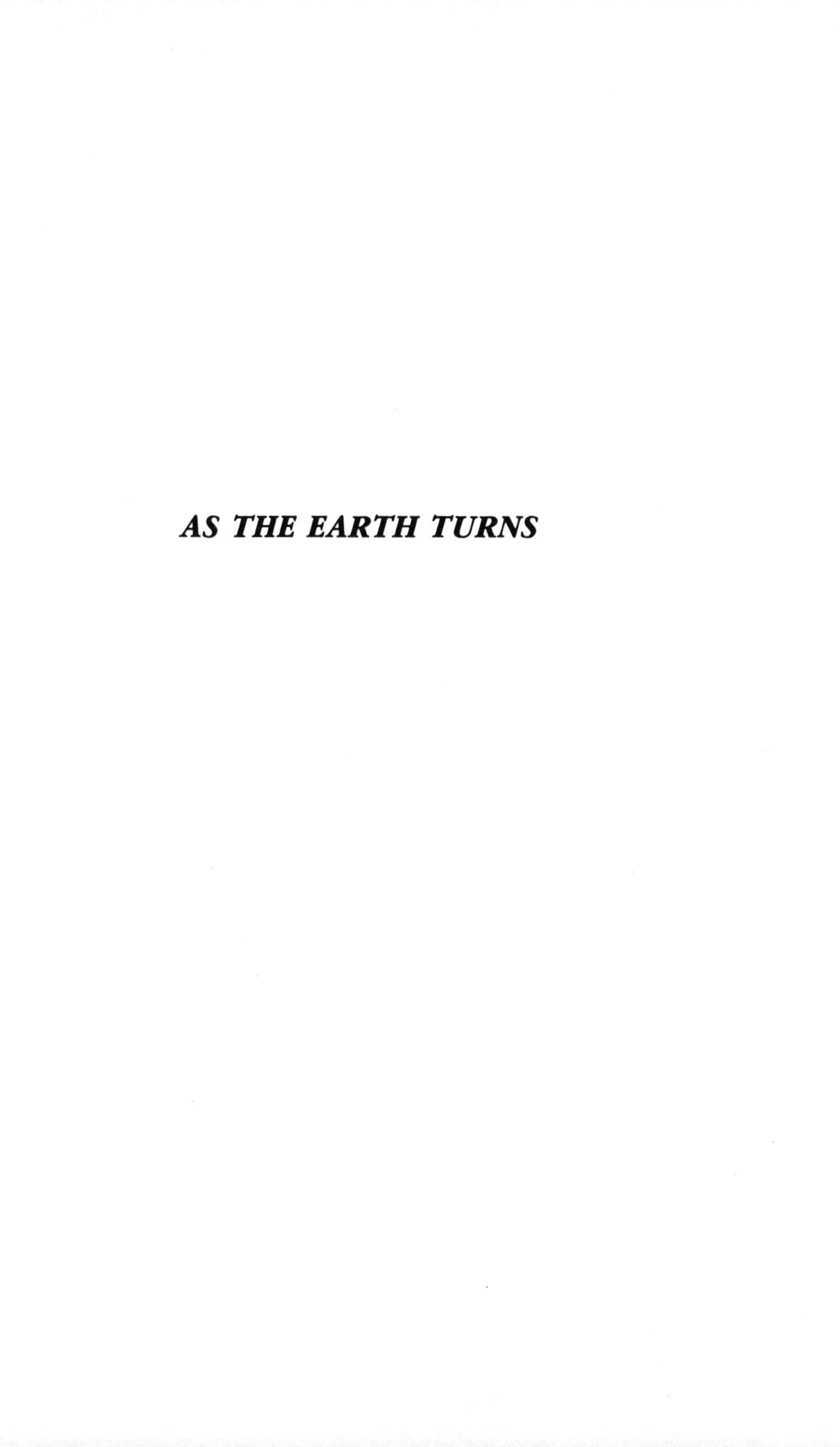

AS THE EARTH TURNS

APPLES

Summer has laid
On the smooth grass a tree of shade
Bearing on boughs where never flower was bright
Apples of clear sunlight.

These, winds arrange,
Destroy. But swift before cloud change
The eye takes harvest in and mind has stored
The globed translucent hoard.

Then in the hour
When from the bright ethereal shower
Of pelting radiance, relentless light,
The eye withdraws its sight

Preferring now
The inner landscape's tranquil bough,
Closing the eyelid on the private dream,
The poised, perpetual theme,

The apples lie
Lucent beneath the inner eye
Preserving in that subtle, weightless air
Forever summer there.

ON A GLITTERING DAY

I cannot live with brightness any more.
Let come a cloud
To blunt the edge of light and make the day
Sound not so loud.

Fall night as dark as candle-black and vague
With smothered wings
And dimly flowing water mirroring
Uncertain things.

Be far from me all eager people. Here
Let be a friend
Who lives at ease with silence and upwinds
Its ragged end.

LANDSCAPE, ASHFIELD

That shaking-leaved birch tree, sun-struck,
Moss at its root,
In wild grass bending in wind above this tiny
Flower not bending, tranquil stem of bells;
The slope beyond, mottled with cows, and tinkling,
Saplings beside; and smooth
Correctly beautiful lawn across the road:
These all palpable, sharp,
Piercing the eye with exquisite, separate light,
Are yet in the eye not separate, not unique,
But framed, embraced by sight
As one: landscape perceived as whole.

Let now the mind's mood change, and instant falls
Fragment from fragment, everything apart:
The grass bends singly, bladed plain, the tree
Starts from the moss,
And lawn and slope are strange though eye still
    binds
The light from all in radiant, close sheaf.
What strange cement, what subtle thatch was there,
Serene bond gone?
Dissolved to bright disparities they stand
Like separate stars printing the inner dark
Which cannot comprehend them single now,
Nor knew the clear amalgam made them one.

GREEN WALK

How perilous is walking
Through greenness thick with light
Like water parting at each step
To surge against the sight!

The dazzled leaf, the fennel
Spotting the grass, the thick
Web on the matted brier,
The lichen-crusted stick

Print on the flooded lenses
Till blind the brilliance grows
And on the drowning vision
The inner eyelids close.

Behind those inner curtains
The soul recovers breath,
Revives in darkness from the bright
Luxuriance of death.

So perilous is walking
That only on return
To wall and roof and shutter
Are eyes allowed discern

The million-leafed, the flaunting,
Green, *remembered* tree.
Only in recollection
Is beauty safe to see.

THE VALLEY

Exists, there, this valley, hollowed and rounded,
Shaped to the shaping hills, puckered by trees,
Bearing the white flower of frost in the shadowed
Hour after sunrise, and the frail chimney blossom,
Smoke of farm kitchens. See, over dun pastures,
And red fields folded in furrow, heavy and cold,
The veering poise of buzzards and the undulant
    crows.
Exists, this valley, is ploughed, trodden by horses,
Swift wheels and the feet of men; is seam in the
    hand,
Dust in heaped nostrils, dark alloy of snow.

But clear, exact, complete, behind the eyes
The imaged valley lies and has no weather
Nor depth nor substance known to fingering sense
Nor sound to startle ear and hill together.
Yet is this counterpart, this evanescent
Mirage and figment, the ploughman's dearest field,
Beyond the corn leaf cherished and the sweet clover,
By him held fast though other fields are lost;
Acres of shadow his estate to hold,
A dream his earth, a shade his map of heaven.

WILD BIRD

Where has the wild bird gone? Where is it flying?
It was here. I saw it an hour ago.
For days I have seen it. I thought the wild bird was
  staying.
Where did it go?

There was red on its wing, but I never heard it
  singing.
I fed it, I scattered rice on the bare ground.
It walked on small feet there where the rice was
  lying,
But it made no sound.

There are bogs, there are marshes, cold, with bright
  berries swaying
In thickets, and fields where the gold grain fell.
To stubble and bog-berry must the wild bird be
  winging,
Ways it knows well.

From crumbs and the scattered rice the wild bird is
  flying.
It was here, but for taste of the wind-strewn seed
And bitter wild berry, for field flight and marsh
  stems swaying
The wild bird had need.

POPLAR BOUGH

Over the window, bough of poplar striding,
From sill to lintel swings
In one long leap across the glass, dividing
With dark impermanent diagonal
The angles of the panes.

With shadow seasonal it moves, eliding
An instant, sparrow's wings
Or the bright leaf of snow, an instant hiding
The glass snared winter stars or aestival
Brown spatter of fly stains
On the hot panes;
And braids unquiet shade with trailing strings
Of light let through the sliding
Green sieve of leaves, or scatters the bright grains
Of glancing rains.

Now from faint sleep the poplar quivering springs
At sound of the wind riding
To far-off hounds; root-held from flight it flings,
In that perpetual leap across the panes,
An arc to freedom, gliding
Beneath an oriole who sits and sings.

THE BEE

Out of the deep corolla of the day
The sun crawls slowly forth, a shaggy bee
That oars his yellow cargo through the sea
Of air and, pollen-brimmed, at every sway
Spills the gold over-freight along his way.

The great hive swallows him. A little while
The furrowed winds run golden in his wake,
Until night brings the herd of stars to slake
Their thirst at the rich furrows. In bright file
They drink, and darkness fills each honeyed aisle.

SLEEP

So sleeps the susurrant wind that the star's leap,
The fiery plunge down dark across the sky,
Evokes no breath more deep
Than wafts one loosened leaf to midnight pool.

So smooth the stillness lies that distant sound
Of bark or cockcrow shatters in one burst,
Then settles to the ground
And disappears without an aftertrace.

So far the light has come, so long the way
From distant moon to curtained window runs,
Only the faintest ray
Glimmers on eyelids and on pillowed hair.

So calm their breathing is, though bodies keep
The attitude of love, turned each to each,
Almost this quiet sleep
Seems slumber in a dream of death's repose.

WATER PICTURE

Sometimes dislodged from a deep niche of sleep
By some cross-weaving current of the night
I float up to the surface of a dream
And waken and lie still a moment there,
Upborne as by a sea that hugely holds
Monsters, and birds asleep, and swimming stars,
And the red husk of a late-fallen moon.
Some memory of the rhythmic underflow
And fluid order of that deep-sea world
I knew in sleep has washed the moment clear.
Dissolved in that bright drop my life appears
Dispassionate, unhurried, free from pain,
Transparent to the deeply gathered core
Where all its conflicts melt and fuse. The trees
Outside my window lean upon the wind
With a low sound of rest. Even the thought
Of you and of that too brief love we had
Holds for the moment no constricting hand
About my heart. I know, accept, and sleep.

NIGHT ENCOUNTER

The reticent porcupine at night
Adventures from the woods. He moves
Across the edge of untreed space
In purposeful slow shamble, black
In larger black of air and ground.
No moon picks out the fainter dark
Of road, but starshine shows the shape
Of ditch and bank and graveled track.
He crosses with no sound. Night-hid,
He boldly seeks the human den
Whose windowed walls, unhostile now,
Are lapped in smell of sleep. He mounts
The deck that runs past screen-barred door
And follows, seeking food. Returns.
Beyond the screen a woman dreams
She hears faint sound of feet on wood
And wakes. Awaits returning steps,
And breathless blinds with instant light
The huddled creature's frozen gaze.
Three feet, a million years, divide,
Hold fast their eyes. The two-way stare
Is moment-long but timeless while
Their two worlds meet and shock apart.
The porcupine withdraws his eyes,
Resumes his hulking progress through
The arc of light and disappears.
The woman gasps, restores the dark.
She moves as from a spell released
And, wondering still, returns to sleep.

EARLY MORNING

The world wakes slowly. Trees begin to stir
And then drowse back to stillness. Startled birds
Cry out to seize the covering night that slips
Down from their feathers slowly to the floor
Of earth still dark but lightening. Too cold
The pale light is for birds to sleep.
They draw the whirring air about their wings
And twist it to bright notes, while squirrels fold
It smooth in leaps along the greening ground
From tree to tree and crackle up the bark.
Pale mushrooms huddle in the chilly grass,
And opening white morning-glories round
To flaring horns that in the still air ring
With unblown, noiseless music. Hanging near,
Between tall stems the taut webs sag with dew
And hidden spiders wait what day will bring.

BIRD IN HIDING

O bird, come near that I may see you singing.
Such stabbings of sweet sound
From ambush run bone through too quick for fending
Before the anguish point of joy is found.

Than ear is eye more wary for the bending
Aside of beauty's spear;
Let me but see you: only sweet sound springing
Source seen is not too beauty-sharp to bear.

APRIL FIRST

Now along streams the willow
Clouds yellow
And foggy green,
But snow lies in the hollows,
And wind is keen.

Now along roads the maple
Looms purple
With fronds of red,
But hawthorn and wild cherry
Look dead.

Now along streets the poplar
Draws farther
From splitting buds
The first wet webs to venture
The windy floods.

In parks now crocus fire
Flames higher
In grass and ground,
But the magnolia taper
Is still unbound.

RAIN

This curtain, this bright cover, drawn to the ears,
Of rushing sound, green water, drops out of heaven,
Shuts out the noisy stillness of the sun,
And the loud moon, intruding, not to be shaken,
The insistent stars, the unavoidable landscape.
All day the rain, all night, has heaped this burrow
Of isolation; and in it, warm, is smell
Of the mind breathing, curled on its dark feet,
At home. In such close chamber the self is large,
Its pulse magnified to significant beat,
Its odor, self-savored, sweet, and sweet the curves
Of its unmirrored shape. By the brief bliss
Of auto-intoxication medicined,
The self regains its health, renews its courage,
Relaxes, flexes; with raised head, ears alert,
It listens, peers, steps forth. The rain has stopped.

LEAF

What meeting of likes, opposites, insistent molecules,
Lines of force converging, was captured here
To form this angled leaf, this pattern of veins and
elbows!
Digesting the sun into greenness, sifting the air
For elements that obey those secret cells
That make trees' blood
By rite and recipe a billion years unchanged,
It hangs immersed in light, held fast in flowing wind,
Moving but never moved.
Till stem lets go. The fallen leaf decays;
Its essences emerge, disperse;
Unbound, the lines of force diverge once more.
But still this elbowed shape
Lives on, a green thought recollected,
Till memory's forgotten landscape grants
A final dissolution.

AUGUST, VERMONT

This green light
Is a smooth-flowing river.
We swim in it like fish
Moving from shadowed coves
Into clear pools of sun.
Above us birds
Dive through the greenness, weave,
Cleave, arrow the liquid air,
Or fin from tree to tree in scalloping spurts.
Leaves dangle,
Awash in invisible currents.
Loosened, a leaf eddies,
Slowly gyrating, angling
Through the green depths into dim
Dapple of leaf-mould floor.
Leaning on light, laved by air
We swim in the green translucence,
Sustained, enfolded, held
At ease, submerged in summer.

THE AMBUSH

The orange lilies wait in ambush
To spring like tigers in a sudden blaze
Of savage color on the unwary
At the bend in the road where the green rays

Of the sun break through the trees to dazzle
The eyes. A moment's startle as the glance
Takes in the tawny splendor poised
By the dark woods in sultry stance.

The impact of the feline flowers
Staggers the mind, which blindingly now perceives
The wild force burning in the grace
Of velvet petals, fragile leaves.

POPLARS

The poplar trees are letting go their leaves.
Out of the green foliage down
And the shivering music that weaves
Them to summer, they fall, yellow and brown,

On the path of the year where the wearying, dust-stained days
Hasten their steps and recall
That poplars see first through the haze
When summer has turned and set her face toward fall.

TO ONE WHO DIED IN SEPTEMBER

I

This is her place,
Between sod and stone
Between dark and dark, with silence
Curved to her bone.

She chose it well
Against winter storm
Against the cold sun; from both now
She will lie warm.

Richly she chose
In her final dearth
To shroud with robe immortal
To wear the earth.

II

Earth has not changed much since you saw;
The green leaf into gold on elm and beech,
Red on some maples, poplars almost bare,
But much green still, and dahlias and the grass
Bright as they were, awaiting the first frost.

And still at the same hour we pass
Down the same streets, still as you were (your hair
Dark, in a braid) remember; but we draw
Leaf-change into our blood, for now we reach
Back for you once abreast, and we take care
That we remember you, lest you be lost.

END OF OCTOBER

Yellow thick the maple leaves blowing and sifting
Lie in curled drifts on the grass.
Wine-leaved the pear, but unleaved already
The cherry, where starlings confer and pass,
Flocking wing-glitter and shadow swooping to
  stubble.
Air snuffs thin and odorous. Shine is heady
To man frost-warned: deep he scoops the sun,
Drinks light, soaks up the gold-pooled shallow
Warmth between shadows, the brightness dark-
  underspun,
Greedy for summer, now the summer is done.

SNOW

Not feather, flight-loosened, has set this downward
snow
The pattern, the pace. Curving mane of seed
Drifting, gyrating, marked no course for the mind
Seeing snow to follow, nor has wind flung pale bead
Of blossom shattering from cherry bough
As now it flings the snow. Not though mind's need
To name and so know the frail, the exquisite thing
Finds in feather, in blossom falling, in seed a-wing

Snow likeness, (finds it even in the faint
Last finger-touch of lover on dead loved)—
No archetypes are these. Too slight, too quaint
The image is that names only the grace
Of snow to medicate the mind's complaint
Deep-seated, mortal, the desire to know
Fully and lose its separateness so.

Deeper than flower or feather sinks the mind,
Haunted and fumbling, deeper, farther back
Along its image trails than these can point,
Seeking confused and blind the ancient track
Beneath all knowledge eye- and finger-sensed,
The body memory, traced when to the rack
Of blood and breath time first was fit and beat
A pattern in the mind with shapeless feet.

Reaching in that dim pattern its own old
First foothold, the mind senses and perceives
Again the effortless slow days unfold
From infancy and flower and pass and pass
Like flakes on the faint wind of years and hold
In their frail sequence what it sought to know,
The endlessness that is the bliss of snow.

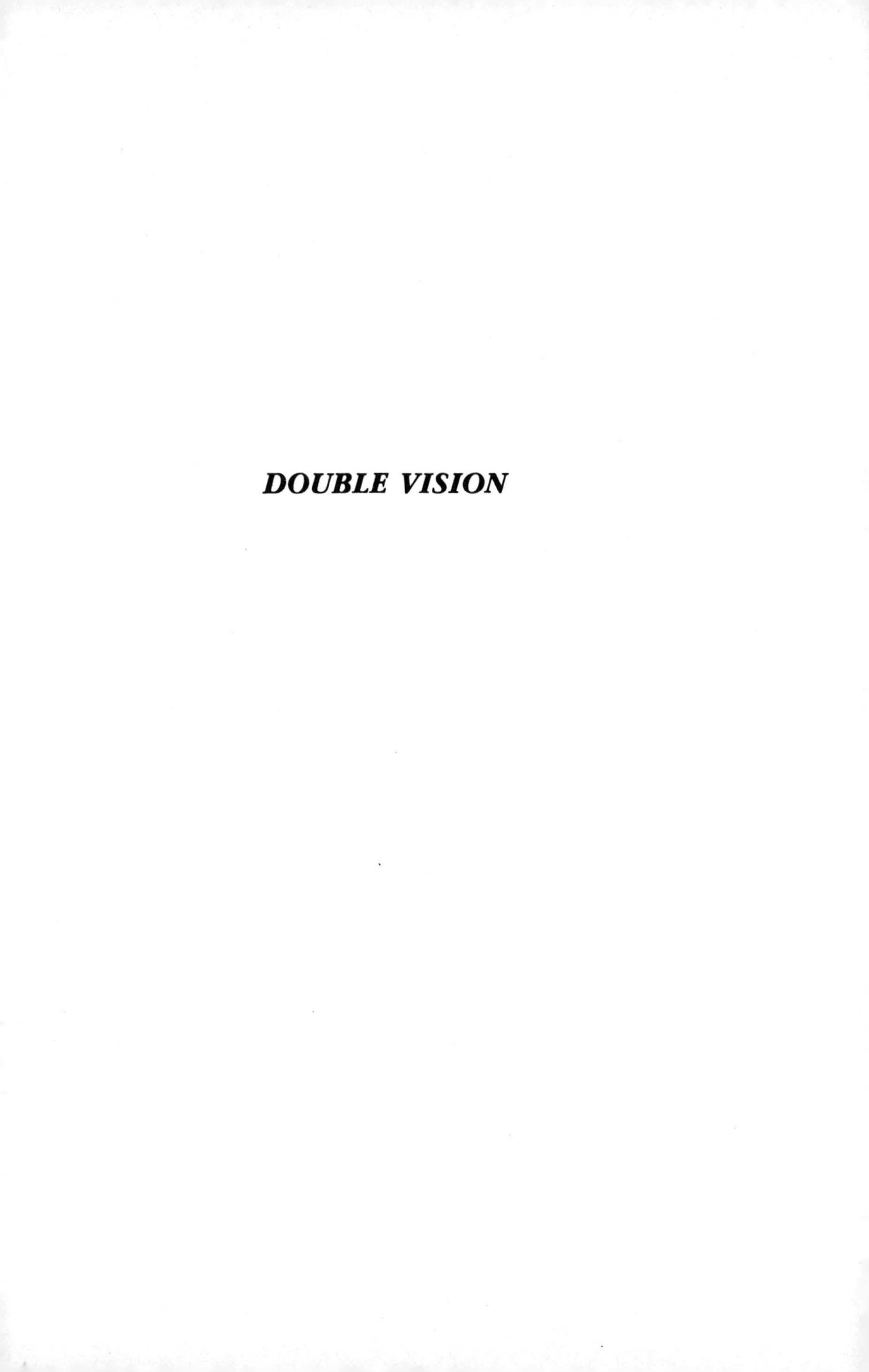

DOUBLE VISION

FROM A PSYCHOLOGIST'S NOTEBOOK

I

The unused hand grows paralysed,
The unused voice grows dumb;
Sometimes mind finds its faculties
Inexplicably numb.

II

To cover its ineptitude,
Disguise its lack of skill,
The mind invents a thousand tasks
It can do well.

To hide its fear of what it can,
It boasts what it cannot;
And resurrects a hundred ways
What it has long forgot.

III

Confronted with the chance to do
What long it has desired,
Dismay assails the mind. It finds
The longing long expired.

IV

The mind so fears to burn
With an intenser fire
Than warms the life to which
Safety permits aspire,

To sharpen and refine
The agony of seeing
To the requirement of
A more exquisite being,

It dulls perception's edge
Till blindness settles there,
And guards its flame so close
It dies for lack of air.

THE MOLE

A poet is a mole who burrows blind
Under the ground, beneath the roots of grass,
Finding his food in darkness, pushing through
His tunnels where the hidden vermin pass.

Our solid ground by him is made infirm.
Under is up to him—inverted sky
Whose dark frontiers he excavates alone
At our foundations as he passes by.

THE WORD UNSPOKEN

Deep in the mind the buried, misbegotten
Word never spoken, cast like fetal foal
Before its time, lies rotting in heavy soil.
Dead, it has life in darkness, breeding dark
Worms that remain unseen but travel far
Under the ground, prolonging to perverse
And poisoned immortality the brief
Survival season of the doubt exposed,
The anger born at term, the fear brought forth
And suckled in the sun. The word unstated
Rings in a subtle subterranean ear
Louder than life and spoken twice as clear.

KNOWLEDGE

Put your hand on the ground; touch grass, touch leaf,
And pebble and hollow of sand
Crossed by pack-train band
Of ants beneath gnats simmering, and high
Shadow-flinging bird. The touched, and the touching
  hand,
The seen, and the glance of the eye,
The earth and the sky—
Such things upon this small and stony star
The mind perceives. But it recoils amazed
From knowledge as from grief,
Its span too tight, too brief
To close on comprehension, stretched though far;
Holds, foiled, one thing as known beyond belief
Though it not penetrate
Perception's spate:
To be of human blood is, racked, to stand
Credulous, by incredible leaf and sand.

IN THE WOODS

Curled
In the dark hollow of the woods, like creature
Startled and still I lay and pricked my ear
Upon the dark pulsation of the world.

Fly buzz, flicker of leaf falling on humus,
Bird,
Booming on log, the wind flowing and falling
Over all sound, beat out the pulse I heard

Moving through root and rock and sifting water,
Through ancient bone and living, under, about,
Around,
The mighty circulation of the ground.

Alike
With that great beat I heard my own pulse run
And knew at last myself to nothing stranger
In wood or creature. I felt that knowledge strike

My life apart to the roots where dim thoughts,
  loosened,
Stirred
And breathed. I saw them trembling rise and heard
Running across my mind their strange wild feet.

POSSESSION

Homage to Emily Dickinson

Postpone the coming of the muse.
Avoid it if you can;
To be possessed is agony—
Mind stretched until its span

Must break or yield electric words
Charged with a force to fuse
A poem into burning shape
Whose lines become a noose

To catch and hold the reader fast
In fierce felicity;
For evidence of agony
Is read as ecstasy!

Then welcome every hour of fire.
Give agony its due,
Grateful that incandescence leaves
Such brilliant residue.

TELEPHONE

The telephone shrills twice, three times,
Then stops. My outstretched hand draws back,
But I am teased. Wrong number?
Or perhaps one tried but shrank
At the last from contact, impulse reined
By doubt that says, "Withdraw, hold back.
Don't risk a word that might reveal
A chink in your wall. Stay safe, stay secret."
The canceled call that might have pierced
That isolation leaves me reft
As well—my wall, like his, unbreached.

AFTERNOON WALK

Petunias flaring in pink corners, the severe fence
  no longer restraining
The gone-away dogs that raced the lawn bare, thin
  grass returning,
And the walk past, remembering the barking and the
  stir of fear
As they leapt at the wire; wondering whether the vet
Or the pound has silenced that ecstasy of noise;
  finding the air
Paler now it has lost the bright blood of their joy.
The silence echoes from the fronts of appeased
  houses,
But what is lost glares from the neighbors' doorways,
Seizes a moment by the throat for instant resurrection
Of a time inhumed in the frenzy of barking dogs.

THE DISCOVERY

I have fastened my windows and closed my doors.
Safe am I from dread
Of that which seeks to come within
When I would sleep in bed.

I will not listen, I shall not hear
That voice that names my name,
And I shall laugh and lie composed
Rid of fear and shame.

I shuttered the windows and barred the doors.
No voice called without.
But in the lull I heard my heart
Give the same voice out.

HYMN TO PAIN

Oh Pain, for this thy hymn I'll sing of joy.
I would not ever, could I, thee destroy,
But in thy honor these my words deploy
And thus defend thee.

Without thee, Pain, delight would disappear.
No birds would sing hosannas in my ear.
Never would joy or ecstasy come near
To bless and rend me.

For joy is measured by degrees from pain,
And with thee gone what measure would remain?
Since bliss needs agony I must retain
Thee to attend me.

Discrimination, difference, degree,
Contrast, variety arise from thee.
For these thy gifts I'll gladly pay thy fee
If thou befriend me.

Though when thou comest I thee disavow,
My weakness passes with thee. Hear me now
Praise thee and thank thee, Pain, that thus dost thou
Thy presence lend me.

DOUBLE VISION

I see, but what I see
Is less than makes this mountain, less
Than shakes this tree.
Leaf greenness fills my eyes
But those deft cells that snare the sun
And photosynthesize
Leaf shades—blue spruce,
Nasturtium, cypress, willow, fern—
I guess, not see. Behind rock face
Is hid the boil and thrust of atoms.
A world surmised
Revealed by sight that needs no eyes
Surrounds, upholds, and molds
The surfaces my eye beholds.

EAR AND EYE

Cunningly made are eye and ear;
They witness much; they see and hear.
Though they lie in wait, though they do not stir
An inch or a foot, they travel far.

In the prick of light through its hole the eye
Sees earth bulge up against the sky,
And the swollen sun break through and hover
Not long, above till the earth smooths over
And closes firm under grass and water
And the shifting weight of ant and otter;
Sees unstill tree and moving train
And house and bed and sheet where stain
Of death or love or birth is pressed;
Sees limbs naked or gaily dressed,
The twitching muscle, the smirk, the frown,
The line unwitting written down
In the flesh, and the aimless moving hand.
At last the eye from its colored band
Sees the disc of the sun grown flat and thin
And the narrow crack the sun drops in.

The ear marks well how the flowing air
Like water inundates its lair
With waves that fluctuate and break
On its membrane and faintly make
A fainter sound than water creeping
Slowly upon wet sand, or seeping

Through moss and sod, or make a sound
Like cataracts falling on rocky ground.
Within the river of air is set
Ear's spiral-twisted, small-holed net.
It seines the lithe, the quivering note
From bobolink or blackbird throat.
It snares the cry of men and cattle,
The scream, the kiss, the brief death rattle,
And the Protean-spawned, the current-stirred,
Agile, slippery, sightless word.

Cunningly made are ear and eye.
They witness much. They are keen and sly.
But the inward eye and its fellow, ear
Are cunninger still. They see and hear
With craft so subtle they can find
The tortuous pathways of the mind
Through its dense foliage strangely growing
From wildly strewn, haphazard sowing.
The eye can see beneath the scar
The unhealed gaping wound of war,
Discern the fury in the smile,
The innocence beneath the guile.
The ear can hear what the deep heart utters
When the pulse leaps or the voice mutters,
And hear the unsaid words that crowd
A silence till it cries aloud.

Inner and outer, they together
Sense innermost and outmost weather

And interbind in steadfast knot
Outer silence and inner shout,
Solid image and mirrored twin,
Twain into one, without, within.

ASPECTS OF LOVE

THREE SONNETS

I

April is green in all the hedges now;
The first blue violets disturb the grass;
And earth breaks black and cold above the plow
Of pale shoots furrowing where the sun's tracks
pass
Most deeply hooved upon the rain-moist ground.
This is the month of love, when wild things mate
And life renews once more and makes abound
All things that through the winter sleep and wait.
Dearest, my heart is watered earth that breaks
To let a growing love come through from roots
You planted long ago. The sap that takes
The sweet, strong juice of earth to fragile shoots
And budding branches runs within me too,
And makes me green and blossoming for you.

II

Take from its cleft beneath the arching bone
The wedged medulla, or remove the cord
The brain lets down to web the skeleton
With sentient flesh, and the throat's little hoard
Of breath is spent forever in one sigh.
Or take the jetting heart out of its hole,
And the red stream that swelled the veins goes dry;
The body houses with the worm and mole.
But take that dearer than the heart or brain,
More vital than the cord, and interlaced
More deeply in the flesh than fringing vein
Or channel that the flying breath has traced,
Take love away, and tortured, crippled, maimed,
We go on living whom death should have claimed.

III

Through many nights my hands have come to
  know
Your body well. They have explored and traced
Each fold and contour, learned where sinews go,
And how each limb and where each bone is
  placed.
They know the spot where heart gesticulates
In throat and temple when love urges much,
And they have found the places where love waits
To be discovered at their instant touch.
But though from flesh, and bone beneath the flesh,
My fingers find your body's secret out,
Unpenetrated, unfamiliar, fresh,
Your self remains. Housed in and walled about
By tissues measured, mapped, precise in range,
You are unknowable, apart, and strange.

BRIDE'S SONG

Oh love, the time is ripeness,
My life is at o'clock
The hour is fruit, is flavor,
The bird is flock.

Oh love, the time is rightness,
The hour is tide, is full,
The rose is gathered honey,
The forage, wool.

Oh love, the time is richness,
The hour is singing flute,
The corn is heaped in harvest,
The blossom, fruit.

Oh love, the time is marriage,
The day is golden shine,
The hour is consummation,
The grape is wine.

Ah love, your breath is richness,
Your mouth is rose to greet,
And I am ripeness, rightness.
Oh here, Oh sweet!

WEDDING DAY

That was ago and the light then a slant-wise
  October,
Smooth in the afternoon, soaked soft in leaves,
Steeped in yellow deeper than daffodils, gold into
  brown.
The season was fruition, yet was spring,
For time was double, was a double ring
Winding in circle fluctuant but fused
The arrogant infant and the suppliant child,
Laughing and ululant, furious and mild,
The lustful novice and the innocent maid
Eager and hesitant, hopeful and afraid:
Backward the blossom to the laden tree,
Forward the myrtle to the bank of snow.
And the lover salutes the beloved: "I remember
Everything in your kiss, but nothing remains,
For all is together, is one, and I am I,
The separate caught and tied, the circle closed."
The beloved salutes the lover: "Now I remember
The memories I lost and the burning dream,
The womb's embrace, the mouth's long hungering,
The swelling breast, the feather's slow descent
From the birds' coupling, bee in trumpet flower,
The moon's invitation, water's long reply.
For love is above and below and without and within,
Spring in October, bloom on the fruited bough,
And time is backward and forward, under, above."
The ring was every way. For the time was love.

THE DANCE

The stage is set, the scenery in place—
A modern backdrop, with an ancient lawn
And hoary trees depicted on the wings.
A creaking pulley hauls the curtain up
Upon two dancers entering hand in hand,
Their cue the marriage lines intoned off stage.
Advancing, confident, they pirouette,
Correctly bow, correctly win applause,
Then suddenly separate, the man to rear,
The woman front, as though propelled apart
By some centrifugal force beyond control.
And now duet in frenzied counterpoint
Of alternate advance, retreat, pursuit,
Uncertainty, hope, terror, with desire
Tying the pair in moment's ardent pause
Of bent embrace, then urgently apart.
But now the tempo changes. Slower now
The separate search, the passionate recoil,
Until the woman humbly bends, the man
Flings her aside, she begs, he turns away
And she withdraws in anguish. He who spurned
The suppliant approaches her once more
In grave encounter; she not humble now
Moves off with him in equal pace. The theme
At last is stated, and each dancer weaves
The statement into clarity, defines
Himself against his consort, by degrees
More freely moves within his own design,

Embroiders and interprets, with each step
And gesture fortifies his partner's role,
Enriches and reveals the pattern. Now
Together is apart, apart is bound
Together, force and flow, is held, is free
In dance unending till the curtain falls.

ONE YEAR

Memory of valley lying west, always
From windows, from porches, under the downward
  eye,
The bent look like urgent bee clinging
To clustered farm and wide corolla of fields
And the long stem of hills. Never can eye
Suck enough sweetness from that quiet flower
For our starved hives. We shall be always hungry
For honey of space, and feed on this flower forever.

Memory of birds: the frequent sparrows;
That gray bird, svelte singer, catbird; wren
Tail tall, staring; robins; and all those
Wild throats, invisible singers. But oh wings
Of wonder, the dark ease, spread searcher,
Vulture over the valley, with no motion
Perceptible moving, the wingtip feathers apart,
Ailerons balancing this subtlest pilot.
He too on space depends. And space reveals,
A moving focus who creates dimension
And measures for us its impalpable canyons.

Memory of weather: the winter morning
Waking in frugal light, from drowsy bed
Lifting the lids on sunrise; sky at night
Hung on the prongs of stars; the August sun
Flattened on westward hill below red clouds

And sharpening moon. And the weight of cloud on
the skin
Leaning against us in a two-day's fog,
Till wind, and the cloud divided against the breast,
The sky lifted, the sky moved over, the hills pushed
back,
And the eye built space again and retrieved its sight.

Memory of speech that was parturition
For feelings too long carried, brought forth in labor
And pain like death. Delivered, the body of love
Was shapely again, scarred, but ampler for living
And we made test once more of its completeness.
Person and person, separate by the space
Words put between us, we explored this new
Difficult, separate way, discovering
We'd made love breathing room, and learning
That space unites, separation unifies.

SINE QUA NON

It is not enough to love, for the beloved,
Loving too, has no need for the lover's heart,
But that which springs from love, the priceless
  condition,
Is at once its flower and food, its end and start.

It is lightness of heart and hand, it is graceful
  touching;
The heavy embrace is stifling to the soul.
Only the body may clasp in consummation;
The loving heart must greet and withdraw, whole.

TO AN UNBORN CHILD

I

Close you lie, child,
Folded and curled
Out of the light, the blowing,
Out of the world.

Earth, the bright air,
Fire unknown,
Of all the elements, native
Water alone.

Water your warm web,
Wrapping you round
In your undream, unbliss of
Presleep profound.

Secret you lie, child,
Womb-circled bud,
Swinging in soft, your tiny
Cradle of flood,

Stirring within that
Island of sea
Waves when you move that beach and
Echo in me.

II

Milkweed pod is bursting wide,
Silkfoot seed is snowing,
Lulla, lulla, little one,
Wind is blowing.

Stem is brittle, leaf is dry,
Winter berry glowing,
Lulla, rest you warm, my child,
Frost is showing.

Bird is going, bird is gone,
Stream is chill-ly flowing,
Lulla, sleep, the winter storm
Still unknowing.

Seed from pod and bird from nest.
Child in womb long growing,
Lulla now, you too will soon
Forth be going.

WINTER LULLABY

Leaves cling still to the holly, the dark
  rhododendron,
Burnished, unfading, green;
Sun, gone summer will come again, baby my
  darling,
Summer so green.

Snow lies thick, and laced by the feet of sparrows
Under the dogwood trees.
Birds, sweet singers will come again, baby my
  darling,
Birds to the trees.

Red haws hang on the briers, the dark bushes
  dangle
Flame berries stiff with seeds.
Bloom, bright blossom will come again, baby my
  darling,
Flowers from seeds.

Squirrel curls in the tree trunk, mouse in the
  burrow,
Warm in a windless sleep.
Lie here warm from the winter, baby my darling,
You too asleep.

NATURE LESSONS FOR A SMALL BOY

I
LOOK AND LISTEN

Little son, do you hear that sound?
That is Robin, there,
Sitting on the maple bough and singing.
His song slides down the air.

Little son, do you hear that sound?
That is Locust. Where
Under the leaves or grasses is he hiding?
His singing shakes the air.

Little son, do you hear that sound?
That's Bumblebee. Take care!
Don't touch him hanging on that flower, drinking,
Then zooming through the air.

II
ALWAYS MOVING, ALWAYS STILL

Something is always moving,
And something is always still.
The big earth turns around the sun,
But the rocks don't shift on the hill.

And the clouds go softly, slowly,
But the sky is always there,
And the mountains never wander
Under the wandering air.

The birds fly over the valley.
They swoop and soar and glide
Over the motionless houses
And the barns that stand beside.

The roots of the plants are quiet
Although their tops bend low,
And milkweed silk sails high and far,
But the milkweed pods don't go.

Twigs in the grass stay moveless
While grasshoppers leap and whir.
Something is always quiet,
And something is always astir.

III
THE PRIMARY COLORS

Yellow

The yellow sun gives colors to all things—
Green, russet, orange, blue—
His own hue sometimes, as to daffodils
And hearts of daisies, lemons, honey, pears.
Small butterflies are yellow, yellow too
Canaries, but the wild one, goldfinch, wears
Black on his head and tail and bright black wings.

Blue

Blue is a color changes while you watch.
Sea water turns pale green or purple dark,
And sky goes cloudy gray or indigo,
Like people's eyes. For blue bears the soul's mark
More than the other colors, and shifts and turns.
But flame blue's constant, robin eggs will show
The same blue till the shell breaks, and color burns
Steadfast in larkspur and in turquoise stones.
Look for grape hyacinth wild in a meadow in spring,
And the glittering small blue shard of a beetle's wing.

Red

Red is body color, color of blood,
And the blood sees it too, when the eye sees,
And feels it rich and warm in fruit and flowers.
Geranium, poppy, strawberry,
Tomato, cherry, cranberry,
Sumach and maple leaves in fall,
Bittersweet, rose haw, ivy on wall.
The red bird you see flashing through the trees.
That's cardinal, that wears a crested hood.
And in the sky when the bright bird's asleep
Antares sparkles and the planet Mars,
Keeping red fires among the paler stars.

IV
SNAKE

In patterned gold his scales are laid,
With coral band or amber braid,
Or green as grass he moves along,
Or crawls as black as tree he's on.
No voice has he, no liquid note
To call his love, no growling throat
To warn that here a serpent is
But only rattling tail, or hiss.

A snake is hot and cold by turns.
When sun is hot, with heat he burns,
When frost is iron on the ground
He's cold as is the air around.
Beneath a rock he sleeps through storm
No inner fire to keep him warm.
But though no fiery blood has he,
Like liquid fire his bite may be
When burning from his hollow fang
The venom drips and writhing pang
Runs with the poison through the vein
Of that unwary one he's slain.
But poisonless his brothers go
Who swallow or embrace a foe.

No legs support his long backbone.
He crawls upon his ribs alone,
And from his lidless unclosed eye
He sees the mouse go slipping by,
Secret as he, who is by nature
A sinuous and furtive creature.
And when he wearies of his skin
He crawls away and leaves the thin
And hollow husk, transparent, frail,
That held the fury of his tail,
And basking, coils in brilliance fresh
His undulant and scaly flesh.

V
THE PRISONER

Day after day the newt lies on his rock
In stillness without motion. Sometimes stirred
He lifts his head and listens, takes three steps
With palpitating throat and upright head,
Then lowers his frog-yellow belly down
Between bent knees upon the rock again
In hopeless torpor, tail curved back, front legs
Akimbo, thrusting feet like tiny hands
Inward beneath his head, while back feet spread
Two leaves of delicate membrane on the rock,
Ribbed with four toe-spines in a partial star.
Prodded, he plunges wildly from his perch
And waves through water faster than a fish,
Scrambling along the glass wall of his tank
To find a hole a newt may hide in, dark
And small. The spasm of search that lasted one
Aquarium length and breadth is brief. Too soon
He turns and mounts the rock, his safety now
Only to settle there and move no more.

LETTER TO A DAUGHTER

Now I know it is not as long as it once was
Since those old years when you were a folded, furled
Beloved parasite, invert and suspended
In that peculiar liquor the womb distills,
And shook me with turnings; then pivoted the sills
Of my body's doorways in anguished, relentless exit;
So that soon with running feet you would headlong
  follow
Your arrowed gaze to its random target, bold
To finger and fondle what pinioning sight might hold;
Fast then to take all trails of sight, sound, sense,
Learning at last to venture the farthest forest:
Avid, insatiable huntress stalking the world!

Seeing at times the quarry turn and rend you
I wept, invoked the forest to be fair—
Meadowed and flowered, thicketed with cherry,
Where lurked the deer, the squirrel, and the bird,
But never wild boar laired or panther stirred.
Ah, but you marked my tears, inferred the tiger,
From the attempted calm deduced the terror.
Wiser than I, you have known to seek where fears
Pinpoint the hunted, silence assaults the ears.
Innocent and intrepid, you wear your wounds
Like the years that have passed, sure now your
  danger lies
In safety, and *I* the enemy to beware.

To read myself as enemy needs a learning
That's hard to come by. The alphabet's not taught
That spells me to myself. Now the slow scholar
Must con the deep-writ language of blood and bone,
Must read the sentence before the words are known,
Infer the meaning. That early day I bore you
I thought was the only, the final parturition,
Not knowing that birth costs always a double price:
That every mother must bear her children twice,
Once from her body's womb, then cast them forth
From enwombing love. Go then, my twice-born
  huntress,
To follow what trails you will. Your freedom's won.

FAMILY PICTURE

They stand on the faded lawn in yellowing line:
The smiling youth with his dog; a daughter there,
Plump and sullen with fan; the mother stands
Composed and smooth in black with folded hands
Near the father seated in center, bearded, benign;
Then the tall, prim girl with a book; last the hired
  man,
Tight and proud at the head of the prize brown mare.

Behind the glass like butterfly impaled
The mounted moment hangs upon the wall,
For fifty years as when, with posture tricked
To artful ease, breath held, the shutter clicked,
And the net flashed, the thing was caught, the bright
  wings jailed;
Imprisoned time pinned to a camera plate,
Displayed in sepia to the gaze of all.

The lens has caught too much and not enough.
Beneath the glass no eye can now discern
What made the smooth wings beat—what current ran
Between the grass the dog the horse the man,
Compelling with affinity so tough
That these, of all the world, drew close and made
This moment a photographer's concern.

Under the gesture pinioned by the fan
The desiccated flesh shrinks into dust,
The smile is stiffened into grinning bone,
The folded hands lie locked beneath the stone,
The horse rears to a phantom that once ran
In legend, and the dog melts into grass
Without a trace save one spring's greener thrust.

Only the features and the attitude,
The gesture and the trappings now remain.
But these were made by motion and by heat
And circulation of delight whose beat
And flow made man and creature share one mood.
That flow was moment's life, essential time,
No net can capture and no glass retain.

OLD AGE
THEME AND VARIATIONS

THE FINAL SEASON

It is time to loose
The leaves of life's long summer.
That green luxuriance is a burden now
When the landscape slants to the north
And the sun grows meager.
The years command: Divest;
Be spare, be single,
Let the leaves fall.
Meet the final season
Bare-boughed, your pattern clear
Against the cold, late sky.

ST. VALENTINE

What has that ancient saint to do with us?
Concerned with dowries for impoverished virgins
He had his eye on youth and its encounter
With love. He viewed the lovers' declaration
And wedding knot as his most urgent care
And gave no thought to what came after. Love
Continuing in marriage was beyond
His interest. We found it must be nurtured
And tended by ourselves. But rooted deep
It proved no tender plant but sprung from wild
And hardy stock, at home in heat and frost.
Quarrels and partings, failures, bitter words
Could not destroy it; after fifty years
It flourishes. No matter we are lame,
Forgetful, deaf, arthritic, growing stiff
In mind and muscle, of ourselves unsure,
We know beyond all doubt love is alive
And bright between us, indestructible.
So on this lovers' day I proffer here
A valentine in praise of the long love
By marriage fostered, by the saint unguessed
As aftermath of moments that he blessed.

ONCE MORE THE SUMMER

Once more the pilgrim earth returning
From voyaging around the sun
Has passed the equinox in season
And brought the summer in.

Across the land the green fire burning
Ignites on bush and tree and hill
And crests in full-blown leaves that burgeoned
From buds they slept within.

Once more the August winds are churning
The tattered leaves of summer's prime.
Once more the cloudless stars will witness
September's frosts begin.

And soon the autumn eye discerning
The red leaf fall, the gold turn brown,
Will mark the snow beneath the birches
Where light lies cold and thin.

And autumn hearts each year relearning
How fast the seasons peak and pass
Take comfort in the ageless sequence
That goes and comes again.

Once more the pilgrim earth is turning
Toward solstice and the lengthening days,
And on its course in proper season
Will bring the summer in.

ON ENTERING OLD AGE

Be glad that youth is gone, for only now
In age can you look back and see the shape
Of your own life and trace the where and how
Of ways you went, the pathways of escape
Not taken, endings that you now can know.
Savor the wine pressed from the tangy grape
Your own sparse fields have lately learned to grow.

Be glad that you are able to forget
So much your avid memory once possessed.
Let self-forgiveness cancel out regret;
Time forgets all, your errors with the rest.
Cherish the hours of joy you'll gather yet.
Be curious still. Accept that at the last
Death is a certainty, fear the only threat.

THE LOOK OF FRAGILITY

In age the look of fragility may be deceiving,
For the old are tough; resilience is their virtue.
They have survived the battles with disease
By learning how to read the body's language,
Observe its rules, and medicine its needs.
Having outlived ambition and cast off
The nine-to-five addiction, now they build
Contentment on diminished satisfactions.
Old loves, old hates are cud for present chewing,
Proof of rich pastures in a bygone summer,
But savored still when rolled upon the tongue.
They draw their lives about them to keep warm
Through the long evening, content to nurse
A smaller fire than burned on former hearths
And close off one by one the unused rooms
They furnished long ago. They have learned
The comforts of restriction and the enhancement
That scarcity confers on meager joys.

THE PASSIONATE SEASON

Old age is a passionate season, though the old
Dissemble lest observant youth should mock.
Old flesh still knows the body's paths to joy,
Still yearns to speak the unspoken language
Of carnal comfort only lovers know.
But there's another passion burns in age,
The fierce desire to understand at last
The human destination, know before
Death puts an end to knowing, how we arose
On this engendering earth and why we're patterned
With the need to find a meaning in all patterns.
Beneath their outward calm the old live lives
Tempestuous with joy or rage, impatient,
Curious, fearful, swept by grief or pain
Alike as those who daily pass them by,
A younger version of the aged they'll be.

THE CENTENARIAN

I have survived my enemies,
Outlived my friends, outwitted death
A dozen times, but now
I weary of longevity.
I am a guest who's overstayed
My invitation to a lifetime;
A quaint anachronism, eyed by the curious,
To whom I communicate nothing; a relic beached
Above high water mark
While the tide rearranges the sands below
To form a different coastline.
A man should die at the right time
While he is still a piece that fits his own puzzle.
My picture long ago was disassembled
And put upon the shelf, and I,
Left over, fit no new design
But one that has the name irrelevance.

THEY SAY I'VE LIVED TOO LONG

They say I've lived too long
The old man said,
But I've a reason still
To lift my head.

I may be paralysed
And forced to lie
All day in this foul bed,
But I'll not die.

I'll spite them all and live
Another year.
No matter that I cannot
See nor hear.

For to exist is why
All men are born.
The mind may be confused,
The body worn,

But life itself's the thing
To have and hold,
Not to relinquish just
Because you're old.

Living I know I'm something,
Though who knows what,
But dead I'll be a nothing,
A meaningless naught.

And who would trade something for nothing?
Not I, not I.
I'll hold onto life till at last
I've no choice but die.

OLD WOMAN'S SONG

I may be old, unlovely to the eye
Of one who looks for pointed breast,
Smooth cheek, inviting thigh,
But what of that!

My mouth was honey and my taste was sweet
To more than one when I was young
And love my heart's own beat.
And what of that!

I've lived my life and loved it. What I had
Was worth each bit of what I paid.
And should I now be sad
Because of that?

I'll not cry because no bright tomorrows
Repeat my yesterdays. I've found
Old joys appease new sorrows.
And that is that!

CONFRONTATION

Suddenly from a letter tumbles out
A photograph of fifty years ago.
I stare at the girl that sits on the grass half smiling,
Her gaze bent to the flower in her hand,
Her full cheek lit by the sun—my youth laid out
On the desk before me. Such innocence
Ought not to be preserved to challenge age,
Which knows how innocence was lost. The picture
Burns my hand. Beneath that tentative smile
Lay all the miseries of a fifteenth summer:
The exquisite shame of awkwardness perceived,
The fear of what was longed for, sweet dread
And anguished expectation. But she was sure
The answers would be found to all her questions.
She would not know me now except with pity
For withered flesh, nor recognize the point
I've come to where there are no answers,
Only the questions no one knows to ask.
I have outlived her pain, but I contain
Her hopes within my disappointments. Something
Of likeness binds us still. But now at last
I know I can forget her. Could I choose
I would not live her innocence again.

THE HOUSE REMEMBERED

The house remembered surfaces from the deep
Of recollection, proportioned as perceived
In a child's eye, enormous in its spread
And tall as trees, positioned on a lawn
That fades and brightens as the grass springs up
To capture evening dark or morning green.
The child ago wore the house as snail its shell,
Habitant of a self-secreted mold
That bore his imprint and his early shape;
At last outgrew, departed. Returns in age
To find it crouching on a weedy lawn,
Dwindled by half and elbowed by rundown
Suburban neighbors. The insubstantial house
Of random recollection emerges now
A solid artifact of the imagination
To prove this shrunken house a nightmare image
Dreamed by the present to betray the past
Which the house remembered guards and verifies.

PERFECTION IS FOR TIGERS

Perfection is for tigers, or for bats
Or beavers their designed and natural state.
The muscle shaped exactly to the need
Of action moves with purity precise
To measure leap or wingbeat and to mark
The creature poised in time that knows no past
Or future, but each moment as it flows.
The human creature lacks that mindless grace
And sets itself a pattern of perfection
To serve instead. But now, in age, we know
That such perfection fits only the tiger.
The years have freed us from perfection's yoke
To know that to be human is to be
Sprung from a root that eons deep sent forth
The shoot of imperfection that would bear
The fallible human creature as fabulous fruit.

SPECTATOR

I watch
The trees thrashing
In the gale, their branches breaking,
But trees in travail are a spectacle
That does not tear my heart.

I hear
The rocks cracking
In the frost, their granite splitting.
But I am not moved by sounds of fracture
To pity the rocks' ordeal.

I see
A loved visage
In old age, by pain assaulted,
And I am tortured like the breaking trees
And riven like the stone.

AN OLD MAN ANSWERS DYLAN THOMAS

No, Dylan, you don't speak to me.
"Do not go gentle into that good night . . .
Rage, rage against the dying of the light."
That is your youth that cries its terrors there.
That is a youth's bravado you implore.
I rage, Dylan,
But not against that final steep descent.
I rage against
That deep betrayal, myself against myself:
The cell's refusal what the will decrees;
The stiffened joint, the dimming eye, stopped ear,
The slow decay to incapacity.
I rage against my mind's diminished arc,
The drawing in of my circumference.
I rage that daily I myself prepare
And must behold my own indignity.
No, Dylan, you don't speak for me.
I shall go gladly into that good night.
I shall be freed by the dying of the light.

WHAT IF?

The bird, seeking its tropic garden,
Measures a half a world beneath its wings,
Impelled by knowledge bred into its veins
And hollow bones that warns it must depart
And sets its urgent course by sun and stars
Unswerving over landscape far and strange.
The crab, buried in sandy burrow,
Has knowledge of the moon that pulls it forth
Precise to forage with the fluctuant tides.
And grunions time their mating by the moon,
Knowing in moonless seas when to come up
And spawn upon the beaches. Creatures who
Are tuned to the earth's music, or the moon's,
Know when the time is ripe, is right, and move
With sureness to fulfill their life's design.
But man, marking that creature sureness,
Longs for the music that he cannot hear.
His body has no clock that keeps earth time,
For human time is set too fast to match
The slow, unhurried pulse-beat of the earth.
What if in age we also could receive
A deep, imperious signal to depart
And like the bird, within our blood and bones
Be sure *now* is the time! We then could go
With grace and single mind nor cling to life
Too long, when we are too infirm for joy,
And look on death, not as the dreaded end
But as embarkment for a destination
Unknown but dreamed of, never seen, but sure.

SYMBIOSIS

It is death we face, we old,
Over the threshold, near, always in wait.
We know his look. The images arise
Against our will: dead child, the lashes curled
Softly on rounded cheek, innocence
Upon corruption; pestilence-ravaged face
Rouged by the undertaker's obscene art;
And the horror in the ditch, the dog
Buzzing with flies, belly swollen, legs
Grotesquely up. We shrink aghast.
But dissolution, its conditions known,
Is bearable. We fear more what's beyond:
The self erased, the all of nothingness.
Extinction can't be learned. We clutch at faith
But cannot quite believe the myth that death
Sets free the self to rise from outworn flesh
Like the imago from its chrysalis.
But we have seen that death sustains the life
About us and that life creates itself
Perpetually from the death it feeds upon,
Symbiosis strange and comforting,
Assuring that nothing is lost and that in death
We are encompassed by eternal life.

PHOENIX

Bird of love, the phoenix, soars and sings
Never in flame, but when the flame subsides
The glowing embers part above
The wings, the throbbing throat of love.
From age and pain the hidden song arises.
The sagging flesh, the passion briefly spent,
The senses' slackened span are nourishment
For tenderness, the shy bird's other name.
It covers, cares for, comforts, and sustains
The lover and his dear reciprocate
When time runs low and body's hour is late.
The song swells out, the phoenix lifts its wings.

LULLABY

Dearest, lay your hoary head
Here upon my aging breast.
Cradled in my circling arm
Nothing more can do you harm.
Rest, my darling, rest.

Load has lifted that the years
Ever deeper on you pressed.
Let me close your eyelids now,
Fold your hands and smooth your brow.
Rest, my darling, rest.

In an earthen bed you'll lie,
Lapped around in slumber deep.
As the years about you close
Naught can trouble your repose.
Sleep, my darling, sleep.

For the weary there is ease.
There is joy for all who weep.
From all pain there is surcease.
From all bonds there is release.
Sleep, my darling, sleep.

DIALOGUE

Mind says: I'll not give in to age.
I'm just as sharp and sure as ever was.
I'll work and strain,
Hold tight the rein,
And never let my years slow down my pace.
Body says: My members pain.
Relax.

Mind says: I'll not admit I'm old.
I still can do whatever once I did,
Though not as fast
As in the past.
I'll drive the harder to maintain my place.
Body says: I cannot last.
Relent.

Mind says: I cannot longer hold.
The years have overtaken my resolve,
Subtracted from
My earthly sum,
And death has ceased to wear a bitter face.
Body says: The time has come.
Let go.

CELEBRATION

If there are bells, let them be rung.
If there are words of joy, let them be shouted:
Rejoice, rejoice, give thanks.
Give thanks for that first cell that chose
To join with cell, bold for the human venture.
The jetting sperm, the microscopic egg,
The fetal fish
Swimming within the hospitable womb,
Give thanks for these and for the skeleton
That hides the heart behind its latticed ribs
And shelters in its hollow skull
The brain, plump on its armored stem.
Give thanks for body's form, for gift of breath.
Above all, praise the cells' arithmetic
That adds the body's parts
To make a self that's greater than their sum,
That hears and sees and *knows* it hears and sees
And knows itself alive, aware of joy.
Death after such awareness is no pain
And to have lived is blessing.
Sing, give thanks.